WILD ANIMALS

An Animal Information Book

PRICE/STERN/SLOAN

Publishers, Inc., Los Angeles

1984

Squirrels have large bushy tails that help them leap from branch to branch in trees.

They eat nuts, seeds and berries.

During the fall, they find and store enough food to last through the winter.

Wildebeests are also called gnus.

These animals live in Africa in large groups called herds.

Their heads look a little like buffalo heads.

Both males and females have curved horns.

Giraffes are the tallest animals.

They have long legs and very long necks.

Although they can easily reach into trees, they have more difficulty bending down to drink water.

Giraffes live in Africa.

The porcupine is best known for the quills on its back and tail. The quills are very sharp. The porcupine uses them to defend itself against other animals. When another animal gets too close, the porcupine's quills stick in the other animal. The quills are very difficult to remove.

Impalas are members of the antelope family.

They live in Africa.

Male impalas have sharp, curved horns. Female impalas have no horns.

When impalas are frightened, they jump and run very quickly.

Rabbits eat plants and grass.

They usually live in the woods or in forests.

Rabbits have long ears and very good hearing.

When they are in danger, they hold very still or run away.

Elephants are the largest of all animals. They may stand eleven feet tall and weigh six tons.

They live in Africa and in Asia.

Elephants live in groups called herds. There are often ten elephants in a herd, but sometimes the herd is much larger.

Raccoons are very good fishermen and hunters.

They often wash their food before they eat it.

Raccoons weigh about fifteen pounds.

They have bushy tails and black masks around their eyes.

Caribou live in places where the weather is cold.

They have large horns called antlers.

In some places, caribou are used to help farmers work.

These caribou are called reindeer.

Monkeys are usually found in areas that have very warm weather.

They live in jungles, in forests and among rocks.

Many, but not all, monkeys live in trees.

Some monkeys make very strange noises.

Leopards are members of the same family as lions and tigers.

Leopards are smaller than lions and tigers, but they are better at climbing trees.

Leopards have black spots on their coats.

This animal is called a musk ox.

It lives in places where the weather is very cold.

Its hair is so thick that it never gets cold.

The musk ox eats grass and moss.

Frogs have short front legs and long, strong back legs. Their legs help them to jump well.

Frogs have very large eyes and very good eyesight.

They have long, sticky tongues that catch their food.

The buffalo has a very large head and a hump on its back.

It is sometimes called a bison.

This animal lives and travels with a large group of buffalo called a herd.

It is not a very smart animal.

A hippopotamus is a very large animal with very short legs.

Although it cannot walk on land well, it is an excellent swimmer.

A hippopotamus eats the grass and reeds found in and around rivers.